REAL

DOPE

An in-depth comparison between real estate and the dope game

TIMOTHY JACKSON

Edited by SAVANNAH THOMAS

Real Dope

Published by Timothy Jackson
P.O. Box 2071 • Frisco, TX, 75034

Printed in the United States of America

ISBN: 978-0-9973013-0-4

DEDICATION

I would be lying if I said that one person motivated me to write this book. The truth is that various people and situations have inspired me along the way. First, I would like to acknowledge my fiancé Ayanna. She encouraged me to pursue this vision, and she held me accountable throughout the process. She has always believed in me, and has never allowed me to quit no matter how challenging the situation or circumstance. I love you, and I am excited to make you my wife.

I also want to acknowledge my son, William, who is the reason why I get up every morning. Son, I am proud of the intelligent, inquisitive boy that you are, and I look forward to watching you grow up and become a great man! You are my shining star! I love you dearly.

Lastly, I am dedicating this book to my mother Lockie. Mom, you have always pushed me to the limits. You instilled values in me that have made me the man that I am. I have you to thank for my work ethic and my attention to detail. I also thank you for surrounding me with good men in the absence of my father. You knew how important it was for me to have positive, male role models, and your strategic placement of certain male figures in my life positioned me to be successful when faced with adversity. Particularly, I want to thank you for forcing me to have relationships with our family members who were incarcerated due to drug and gang activity. Their wisdom and knowledge, combined with my desire to foster change in our community, motivated me to write this book. I love you, and I know that you are proud of your baby boy!

CONTENTS

INTRODUCTION

Let's face it. A life of crime is more glamorized on television and in mainstream music than a boring 9-5 job down at a local call center. Crime bosses live lavishly, take exotic trips, and throw the biggest parties showcasing their endless cash flow and power. In Hollywood, some of the most polarizing films involve characters that are tied to some type of illegal enterprise, which is associated with drugs, gangs, money laundering, and racketeering. While many love to watch these movies and dream of a life that would afford them the same opportunities, rarely do they actually take the risks associated with the coveted lifestyle.

However, a lot of people are willing to take such risks that will subsequently lead to criminal charges, jail time, or even death. The quick come-up shown in the movies will often omit the grunt work that comes along with the so-called-fame. While people cautiously pursue the street boss or kingpin lifestyle, they often find out that the images portrayed on the big screen are unrealistic. A shootout scene with a local rival in a movie ends with actors being imaginarily killed and a scene change. In real life, that same shootout scene often leads to broken families, jail time, and/or a lifetime of looking over your shoulder. Simply put, a life of crime will eventually come crashing down for the vast majority who dare to take the chance to become a street boss or a kingpin.

What if I told you that you could live like a street boss or kingpin by day and sleep like a baby at night? What if I told you that you could take exotic trips, own immaculate homes, drive fast cars, and have a seemingly endless flow of cash at your fingertips? What if I told you that the true dope game has always been real estate, and you don't need a formal education or a real estate license to be successful or to make a lot of money in real estate? Well, I just told you! All of the above is true. Real estate is the second oldest profession known to man.

Real Dope was written to compare real estate to the dope game, and highlight the many similarities that both professions share. While there are some differences in both fields that will never intertwine, you'll be shocked to learn the commonalties between both professions. One would be surprised to learn how much drug sales and home sales have in common, both logistically and monetarily.

Real Dope is also designed to give you an option to legally achieve the lifestyle and income that you've always desired. Many men in our country, both young and old, are being mass incarcerated at alarming rates due to their involvement with the manufacturing and distribution of narcotics. It is my belief that a person with more financial options will be less likely to commit crimes that will land them in prison or in a grave. By redirecting their attention to a more realistic and obtainable hustle, this will significantly contribute to the reduction of mass incarceration, particularly as it relates to African American men. My mother has always said, "When you know better, you do better!" Education is a powerful tool, and you do not want a decision that you made in your teenage years or your early twenties to follow you for the rest of your life. For those reading this book who have criminal records, you can still have a very lucrative career using real estate as an investment vehicle. There is always hope in real estate. Real estate investors come in all shapes and sizes, and they also come from various backgrounds.

Real Dope is a quick read! It will give you the basics on how to use real estate as a legitimate hustle. What many street bosses and kingpins have in common is that they own a lot of real estate! Real estate provides an easy way to shelter your money while creating tax benefits, depending on the way that one chooses to utilize it. That's right, you can pay taxes on the bundles of money that you rake in from your clientele! Any authentic gangster movie has taught us that most street bosses or kingpins are eventually taken down for tax evasion rather than the heinous crimes that they committed over their careers. With real estate as your investment vehicle coupled with a good accountant (or good tax preparation software), you can keep the Feds off your back and avoid having your door kicked in at 3:47 AM on a Tuesday!

So what's it going to be? As the great actor Denzel Washington said in the movie *Training Day*, "Do you want to go to jail or do you want to go home?" Are you ready to live like a boss and sleep like a baby? I sure hope you are! Let's dive in!

A Product of My Environment

A Product of my Environment

I grew up in a part of Dallas that was not so pleasant, although the name may have suggested otherwise. In Pleasant Grove, you were only as good as those in your inner circle. My neighborhood produced a wide array of individuals, from politicians, attorneys, sports agents, and military officers, to big time drug dealers, murderers, pimps, and sex offenders. Under one roof, it wasn't uncommon to find a schoolteacher, a bus driver, the weed man and a college student. That's just how things were in my neighborhood. The options were endless. What remained the same was the drive of the people and their desire to be the best, no matter their occupation.

The dope game was all around me. My cousins sold and used drugs, the older siblings of my close friends dabbled in the dope game, and I cannot recall a time when I visited my godparents and I didn't catch a buzz from the heavy aroma of ganja smoke that filled the air in their condo. The dope game was at every school I attended, both public and private. While attending a local Christian school from 5th through 7th grade, two of the upper classmen sold weed to students. When I transferred back to public school in the 8th grade, it wasn't uncommon to smell weed in the boy's restroom. Many of my classmates in middle school sold weed, pills, and crack. Needless to say, drugs were all around me!

I knew several people that sold drugs to improve their lifestyles, pay for college, alleviate debt, or to simply blow it off at the club every weekend. It was never my desire to distribute narcotics. I was very familiar with the negatives associated with that lifestyle. I saw too many guys from my neighborhood develop bad reputations that were hard to shake when they finally decided to leave the dope game and become legit. I didn't want that stigma associated with me because I knew in my heart I would be placed in a position someday to change people's lives. The last thing I needed was to have to sue someone for bringing up "allegations" from my past. It wouldn't be a good look in the court of public opinion.

I did, however, want to learn the logistical side of drug sales because I truly believed that there was an alternative occupation where one could experience the same lifestyle of a street boss or kingpin while running a legitimate business. So, I partnered with my friend, who sold weed, to learn the back end of the business. He taught me the business of how to score the weed in bulk, package, and then distribute it. He showed me his techniques for gaining customers, and how to retain those customers. I learned the risks associated with selling dope, particularly getting robbed or going to prison. He taught me how to be aware of my surroundings and to keep my circle small. He said, "A big crew will bring big, unwanted attention! Keep it small and simple and the money will still come." Several of our high school classmates had been pinched for interstate trafficking and possession with the intent to distribute. During the time of my apprenticeship, some were serving federal or state time for their crimes. For me, jail was not an option AT ALL! I had too much to lose, and I was way to skinny and handsome to survive in the penitentiary!

While weed was the drug of choice for must college students, crack cocaine and heroin consumed the older, functioning addicts in my community. One of my close childhood friends knew this market all too well, as he and his comrades had monopolized a particular neighborhood in Pleasant Grove. They were well known and connected in their industry. Still curious about the structure of the dope game, I shadowed this friend as any good apprentice would. I learned quickly that the rules of engagement changed dramatically with different products. This is often the case in real estate, particularly when you compare residential real estate and commercial real estate. This particular friend specialized in crack cocaine, heroin, and pills. He had a very unique clientele to say the least.

Unlike recreational drugs like marijuana that had easier hours and less risks, selling hard drugs was an around the clock job. A dope fiend needed their high, and they were extremely predictable and consistent with their demand requests. Some got high early in the morning, while others got high during lunch or after work. My friend sold crack from 5:00 AM – Midnight or later every single day. When you added up his earned income and the occupational risks that were associated with the job, he made about $8 an hour. However, he always had the cash to finance his flamboyant lifestyle. He worked hard and partied harder. It was not unusual to see him spend $10,000 in a night club or to find him eating at a fancy restaurant where he undoubtedly made the other patrons feel uncomfortable with his loud conversations, and his cold stare downs to anyone who made eye contact with him for longer than two seconds. For him, the money brought power! Power was what I wanted, but I was unwilling to risk my life or my freedom for a little fortune and fame.

There had to be another way. I wanted the lifestyle, but I wasn't about that life! I was way too clean cut to sit in a crack house for 19 hours a day serving fiends. I also was not a fan of potentially going to prison. Both of my friends that taught me the game subsequently served jail time at some point in their careers. It is rumored that one of those friends was often involved in shootouts with his local competition. He was also a person of interest in a few local murders. While those allegations never stuck, the stigma of his alleged actions do until this day. The gangster movies also taught me that there was never a happy ending to this lifestyle. You either ended up dead, in jail, or in Billings, Montana in a witness protection program working as a janitor. For the record, there is nothing wrong with working as a janitor so please don't send me hate mail. I am simply making an analogy that is often displayed in movies when the story line shifts to the person who ratted out the crime family.

I had to find another way to accomplish my financial goals and support my lifestyle. What career could I pursue that would make me a ton of money, have endless product, endless customers, and provided a flexible schedule? Then, it hit me: REAL ESTATE!

THE GREAT COMPARISON

THE GREAT COMPARISON

Real estate is the biggest hustle in the world! Think about it... everyone lives somewhere! Even if you are homeless, you are more likely to live in a homeless shelter than live on the streets. Someone, who potentially receives subsidies from a governmental agency or private donors, owns that homeless shelter. The product and clientele is endless, and the market is ever changing. There are fewer risk involved in real estate than there are with selling drugs, and the products are extremely similar from a logistical standpoint. You don't need a formal education or formal training in either field, and they both come with a "low start up cost."

The lifestyles provided by the two are also quite similar. The persona of success is often on display, and there is a degree of flexibility that comes with both professions. In high school, I had a classmate who seemed to have it all. Her brother played professional football, and her mom owned a real estate company. She wore the nicest clothes, had the newest hairstyles, and was never short on cash. By the 10th grade, she had a newer model car with rims , which added to her popularity. What stood out most about her was the availability of her mother. Her mother always attended games and school events, never looked tired, and always seemed content. Her mother was a very classy lady with the freshest whips! For a lack of better words, her mother seemed to have her stuff together, both financially and socially.

This caught my eye. I always wondered how real estate worked, but I never personally knew of anyone who worked in the industry. I did, however, know a lot of drug dealers who seemed to boast similar lifestyles, but their risk was much higher.

I began to compare the two industries. The following chart outlines the similarities between the two:

	Real Estate	The Dope Game
Location Matters	✓	✓
Endless Inventory	✓	✓
Endless Clientele	✓	✓
Endless Cash Flow	✓	✓
Flip Your Product for Maximum Short-term Gains.	✓	✓
Have a Reliable Connect	✓	✓
Hold Your Product During a Drought and Sell High	✓	✓
ALWAYS Try to Buy Low and Sell High	✓	✓
Deploy Wise Marketing Strategies	✓	✓
Surround Yourself with a Good Team	✓	✓
Know the Market	✓	✓
Know When to Bail Out	✓	✓
Don't Get Greedy	✓	✓
Live Like a BOSS!	✓	✓

When I sat down and compared my options, it was a no-brainer. I had to get into real estate! It was either that or push bricks on the interstate. Real estate could provide me with the lifestyle that I desired and the freedom that I needed. Now that I knew the pros and cons, it was time to dive in and make some money. I was ready to live like a boss!

HOW TO SCORE

How to Score

In order to get into the game, you need money. A good credit score will help, but sometimes you have to use alternative financing to reach your goal. Getting the money is cut and dry. You either pay cash, get a loan through a bank or lender, or buy directly from an owner. This is the same concept in the dope game. You save up to cop a stash, go in with a partner or get the dope fronted to you. Each case presents a different set of circumstances, but the end result is getting the product.

Traditional Loan

A traditional loan is obtained through a lending institution such as a bank or a loan company. You generally need between a 640-680 credit score and about 3.5-20% cash down depending on the loan type. In addition to your cash down, you have to figure in roughly another 3% for lending fees. So all in all, you'll pay between 6.5-28.5% of the sales price to secure traditional financing. Since many of these loan types are insured by the government or private investors, they may come with additional premiums. Due to an excessive amount of defaulted loans during the housing crash that took place between 2005-2010, most lenders now require buyers to pay monthly mortgage insurance premiums that may range between $120-$160 or higher. Your mortgage is lumped into one payment made up of your principle, interest, taxes and insurance (commonly known as your PITI). PITI may vary depending on the location of your purchase, local tax rates, and your credit score. In most cases, the principle and interest will stay the same throughout the life of your loan, unless your loan is scheduled to adjust after a certain period of time. It is common for mortgages to have a 30 year term, but you have the option to structure your loan for as little as ten years or for as long as 40 years. Do what's best for you. Remember, the name of the game is to make money!

Personal Loans

In some cases, you may have to get a personal loan. Personal loans are commonly obtained when the property that you want to purchase is less than $50,000. Many mortgage lenders will not extend mortgages for properties worth less than $50,000. Personal loans tend to have higher interest rates, but they can be paid off like a car note. You may also need collateral and good credit in many cases. Check with your bank to determine what is required of you to obtain a personal loan. Also, you have to be very strategic when applying for a personal loan. Many lenders will steer you towards a traditional mortgage or deny you for a loan if they know that the use of this loan is for the purchase of a property. Be creative and find ways to justify obtaining a personal loan. You may have to obtain several personal loans or have someone partner with you as a co-signer in order to get the total amount needed. At any rate, be strategic and exhaust all efforts before giving up.

Owner Financing

Owner financing is the equivalent of being fronted dope by your supplier. The owner is selling the property directly to you, so the two of you set the terms of the loan. The two of you will agree on a loan term, interest rate, and down payment. In most cases, the seller will want about 10% down with an 8% interest rate. This is common in my area, but it may vary in your location.

Let's do the math based on these estimated figures:

	Lender Financed	Owner Financed
Price	$100,000	$100,000
Term Years	30	20
Interest Rate	4.5%	8%
Yearly Property Taxes	$3,000	$3,000
Home Insurance	$1,200	$1,200
Combined Monthly Payment (PITI)	$856.69	$1,186.44

Notice that the monthly payment is higher when you choose owner financing. The loan term is also shorter, as many owners want to receive their money over a reasonable period of time. Owner financing may be more expensive short-term, but it is an avenue to get your foot in the door with less red tape. Owners tend not to comb through your past like a bank would. You can also lower your monthly payment by putting more money down. Remember, owner financing is less invasive, so a large down payment may not create a red flag like it would with a traditional lender. In most cases, an owner will welcome a large down payment, as this is guaranteed money for them.

For a person looking to transition from a "cash lifestyle" to a more stable and legitimate lifestyle, this may be the best route to go. You may also consider forming a business, which will allow you to use your property as a legitimately structured entity.

Hypothetically, one could form a Limited Liability Corporation (LLC) through their state for as little as $500. They could call it XYZ Properties. With $10,000 down, they can acquire a property directly from an owner through their business name. They could rent out the property and use the income made from the monthly rent to pay off the property sooner (i.e. pay $1,186 in mortgage, charge $1,500 in rent, cash flow $314 monthly). They could then apply the $314 to the principal balance each month to reduce their loan balance at a faster rate. They could also make bulk cash payments directly to the owner over a short period of time (3-5 years) to rapidly pay off the house without raising red flags. Once the house is paid off, it becomes an asset of the business and a seamless transition from a "cash lifestyle" is complete! Now that's Real Dope!

Piggybacking

Piggybacking is using the efforts and assets of another to obtain the benefits that would not normally be afforded to you. For example, if one wants to build good credit they can simply be added to a credit card account owned by someone with good credit. The creditor will report the names and social security numbers of the cardholders to the credit bureaus. Subsequently, the person with little or no credit will build good credit at a rapid pace with little to no effort.

In real estate, the equivalent to this is called a straw purchase. While straw purchases are not typically illegal, lenders may prohibit them. However, people do them all the time! We have all heard of someone joking about their car being in their mama's name!

This same principle can be applied to the purchase of real estate. Hypothetically, a parent, significant other, business partner, or close friend with good credit can finance the purchase of a house on paper, and the third party can pay the loan. If the property is placed on the market for rent, the monthly proceeds from the rent can be split between the two. If the property is flipped and sold, the third party can act as the "project manager" who oversees the production of the flip, and the two can split the proceeds accordingly.

So, lets make it plain. You could find a property that is worth $65,000. Someone that you know can purchase the property using traditional financing. Assuming that this property will be flipped, the two of you can draw up a contract stating that you will manage and oversee the renovation process, and that you will be paid a substantial fee for doing so. 80% sounds like a good number, but you can negotiate your own price. Let's assume that $20,000 is put into renovating the house, and that the house sales for $130,000. The gross profit on the house is $45,000. The straw purchaser will pay you your fee from the proceeds and pocket the rest. You can take your proceeds in the form of a check made out to your business, and duplicate this process to generate an honest income.

All you need is 2-3 good flips to accumulate enough money to finance your own flip! The best part about this is that it's all legit money! Results may vary, but this is not an unrealistic scenario. In fact, it is one that I have personally witnessed. A straw purchase takes a lot of trust and no greed. The person making the purchase may want to keep a larger chunk of the money once they see what you will make. This is why it's important to put the terms of the purchase in writing, particularly as it relates to managing the process of the flip. Find someone that you can trust and who shares your vision. The right partnership may lead to a promising future for the two of you! In the end, the goal is to get into a property. The opportunities are endless once you do. You may not make a ton of money on the first property, but you will gain a wealth of knowledge and experience to position yourself to win in the future.

Now I know what you are thinking: How can I become a street boss or kingpin off of $314 a month? When it comes to rental properties, you have to think long term! Contrary to popular belief, it takes time to become a boss! But once you get on top in real estate, it will take an act of God or some really poor decision to knock you off your game. The name of the game is duplication. The faster you duplicate your efforts, the faster you will build wealth. Like the dope game, there are many ways to make money. Above, I outlined how to get into an income property. We will talk about other strategies to build wealth throughout the book. But at this stage of the game, you have copped your first stash. Now, it's time to move that weight!

Weigh It, Cook It, and Sell It

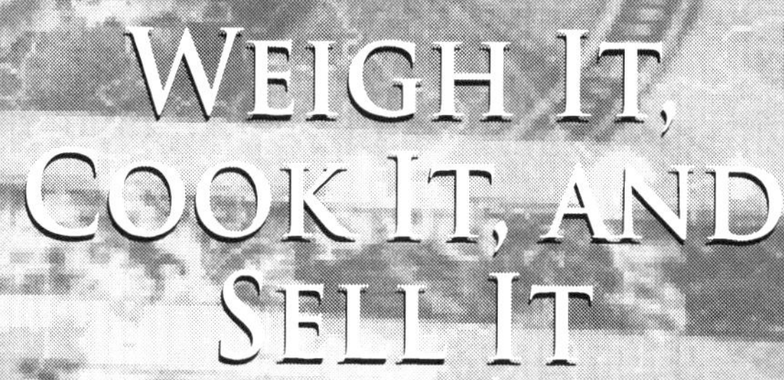

Weigh It, Cook It, and Sell It

Now you're in the game! You have the product, but you need to move it to make a profit. You've done your research, so now it's time to deploy your strategy. The quick money will come with flips, but the long money (residual income) will come when you buy and hold. Just like the dope game, you have to hold some of your product. In a drought, your holdings will keep you afloat. You can sell high and make a larger profit during a drought if you stick to the script. Just like the dope game, real estate has ebbs and flows. There are buyer's and seller's markets. In real estate, many people flop during market changes because they did not have a strategy in place that would provide consistent cash flow during a down market. They over reach or under produce, and it costs them in the end. You won't do this because you're smart!

Flip It

The fastest way to make a profit in real estate is by flipping houses. There is a science to this, and you must know the formula. Like a good street boss or kingpin, you need a squad. You need runners, pushers, cookers, a good location, and of course the clientele. The same goes with real estate. You need a good squad that includes a real estate agent, contractors, landscapers, and potential buyers. You need to buy low and sell high. My rule of thumb on flips is to walk away with a 40% profit. When you are fresh in the game, 30% is not a bad margin. But as you grow your team and learn to cut costs, you will earn more. Remember, duplication is the name of the game!

Using the example from the previous chapter, let's say that you purchase a property for $65,000. The property needs about $20,000 worth of work so that puts your total investment at $85,000. If you sell the house for $130,000, and you contribute 3% to the buyers closing cost ($3,900), and pay 6% in commission (3% to your agent, 3% to the buyers agent = $7,800), your total expenses will be $96,700 ($85,000 + $11,700). You will walk away with roughly $33,300 in proceeds (130,000-96,700). You netted 34% on this deal! Not bad for a rookie!

You don't always have to be in a buyer's market to find these types of gems. Many people are facing foreclosure, and they are willing to sell their property for the remaining loan balance to prevent foreclosure. Since foreclosure notices are public information, you can swoop in and buy the house before it forecloses and potentially make a killing on the back end! This is why you need a good real estate agent who knows how to find these properties. You can also do this research on your own. It may take a little time and effort, but it will be worth it.

Remember, a flip brings fast cash! That cash may vary from a couple of thousand of dollars to tens of thousands of dollars! You can also take a hit if you aren't wise in your decision-making. Don't over reach. If the numbers don't add up, don't do it!

You also must find a good contractor. The last thing you want to do is work with someone who talks a good game but knows nothing about repairs. Check their credentials and view their past work. I once made the mistake of hiring a guy who subcontracted all of his work. We paid him, but he wasn't paying his workers. In the end, we lost a month of production and $3,500 and a lot of pain and suffering. DO NOT TAKE SHORT CUTS ON YOUR FIRST FLIP! Spend the money and make it up on the back end.

Know the market. If the market doesn't dictate flipping, don't flip! Buy and hold! Unless you like fixing up houses and not making a profit, you will be wasting your time flipping a house. Remember, this is about a quick come up. Why place yourself in a risky situation just to say, "Look what I did?" A drug dealer is not going to risk his freedom for the sake of telling great stories at his welcome home from jail barbeque. Use your time and money wisely.

Buy and Hold

Buy and hold is by far my favorite strategy because it creates residual income. You buy the product low, charge a high rate, and put the client in a position to where it won't benefit them to walk away. The best part about buying and holding is that you can use the government to finance your operation! That's right, government subsidized housing (Section 8) is literally the gift that keeps on giving!

Let's use the same scenario of the $65,000 house. We know that your total investment will be $85,000, but your mortgage will be significantly lower particularly if you do a straw purchase or if you get a loan with a low interest rate. Let's assume that the monthly mortgage (PITI) is $600 and the property has 3 bedrooms and 2 bathrooms. Once you completely renovate the house, you decide to rent it out through Section 8. Now I know people hear Section 8 and cringe, but did you know that there are various types of Section 8 vouchers?

For example, I have a tenant who uses a voucher that is specifically designed for former working professionals who are now disabled. This tenant is renting one of my properties located in a planned community with a homeowners association, and she drives a BMW. She has been in this property for nearly three years, and the house actually looks better than what it did before she moved in! But here is the bonus. Since Section 8 typically pays by the zip code and home features (i.e. bedrooms and bathrooms), I am able to charge a higher rate of rent. The beauty of the whole situation is that I don't set the rates! The government does! Her Section 8 voucher covers my entire mortgage. She pays the difference between my mortgage and the rental rate that is approved by Section 8, which is in this case is $350. This is what you call a win-win!

Hypothetically, let's figure out what you would make per month on rent. Using the 75227 zip code and the subsidy voucher chart provided by the Dallas County Housing Agency, a 3 bedroom 2 bathroom home could receive up to $1,100 guaranteed by the government. If the going rent in your neighborhood is $1,300, you can charge the tenant the difference between the two! This is why you hear stories of people paying $200 in rent. So, in this scenario, you would gross about $700 a month! Damn! For an owner financed home, expect to pay a higher mortgage, but you could reasonably gross $500 a month. That's not bad! That's an additional $6,000-$8,400 a year that can be used as a down payment on more owner financed properties! As long as you keep a Section 8 tenant inside, you'll be fine!

In addition to your monthly income, your property will likely begin to appreciate. As you pay the mortgage down, the value of the property is likely to go up, causing you to build equity! If you are smart, you will apply your monthly surplus back into your mortgage and pay off the property faster. Think about it! If the mortgage is $600 and you pay $1,300, you can have the property paid off in 5-7 years, net the entire $1,300 a month and have a property worth $130,000 that you acquired for $65,000! Now, that's *Real Dope*! As always, duplication is the name of the game!

If you really wanted to be crafty, you could refinance the house, pull out all of the cash equity ($130,000), purchase two more houses and repeat the process! Remember the house will be on Section 8, so you aren't paying a dime out of your own pocket towards the mortgage! Now, you have a mortgage that is being paid for by the government and cash to buy more houses! People do it every day! Depending on your area, you could find homes for cheaper than $65,000.

My client purchased 3 houses for a combined total of $50,000 in an area of Dallas that is considered to be economically depressed. He'll collect about $750 a month per house after renovations of about $40,000. He will make all of his money back in 4 years and have the properties with equity to show for it! And the best part is that the government will finance this venture through housing subsidies. It's your time to start taking advantage of a system that is in place for the wealthiest 2%. Congratulations! You've just bought 3 houses in 5 years that are netting you $2,500 a month! How does it feel? This could be you!

With a dedicated team in place, you can position yourself to make huge dividends. Research your area. Consider that old abandoned trap house in the middle of the neighborhood. It may be an eyesore to some, but it's a goldmine to others! You may be able to acquire it by simply paying the tax bill! How dope would it be to actually convert a trap house into your trap house! You bring your own clientele (renters), charge a high rate (Section 8 approved subsidy), and provide a good product that keeps them loyal (be a good landlord)! As you acquire more of these types of properties, those same renters will refer you to their friends and family who also have Section 8 vouchers! Just like dope fiends know other dope fiends, Section 8 recipients know other Section 8 recipients. Take care of them and they will take care of you!

The figures mentioned above may not be typical in your area, but there is nothing preventing you from getting your product from out of town! Like a true street boss or kingpin, you may have to hit the road to make some money. But this trip doesn't require you to get that work from California, nor will you have to fly to Columbia or Miami to score big. You can simply look to a neighboring city or state to find the right product.

Many people own properties in states where they do not reside. This is especially common with service men and women who have had to relocate to another duty station. Instead of selling their homes, they hold on to the property and hire a company to mange it while they are away. Think outside of the box. If you live in California or New York, you may want to consider areas in your state where prices are lower. Sure, a 2-bedroom condo in Downtown Los Angeles may run you a million dollars, but a 3-bedroom house in Mojave may only be $150,000! You may want to consider making a purchase in Texas, Georgia, or North Carolina where the real estate is plentiful and reasonably priced. Seek professional advice before you take this step, but it may be well worth the risk! You have to think outside of the trap! Scared money don't make money!

With either scenario, you will place yourself in a position to make gains. A flip is a quick come up and may potentially yield great dividends. In contrast, buying and holding will bring a slow, steady income. Duplication of both processes will create wealth, and wealth creates opportunity. For you, it may bring a new car, fancy clothes, exotic vacations, and a boss lifestyle. For me, it will bring residual income that can be passed down for generations. Both moves will create jobs, stimulate your local economy, and move you to the next income bracket. Either way, we are both making boss moves! This isn't hard! It works if you work, but you have to want it! Do you want it? Oh yeah? Then let's get it!

What Can Go Wrong?

WHAT CAN GO WRONG?

One thing that has made me successful is that I do not operate out of fear. I am a risk taker, and I know that higher risks yields higher rewards. Like you, many of my ideas were placed on the back burner due to the lack of funds. Once I was able to save up and find a partner to help me invest, my life changed. We took risks, and we made mistakes. However, our mistakes were always overshadowed by our success. I would be lying to you if I said that this is a risk free game. Like the dope game, you will take some pretty scary chances. If you fail, your bounce back game has to be on point, or you will find yourself always taking the passive approach when it comes to making decisions.

Flips Gone Wrong

So what can go wrong in a flip? A lot! Many people fail because they overreach. Some set unrealistic expectations, deploy rogue strategies, and make emotional decisions that may potentially kill the deal. They place more value on the property than it's worth, and they become too emotionally involved when they shouldn't. They expect for things to happen fast, but in reality a flip may take several months to complete and additional time to sell. Always remember that this is a piece of property. Your end goal is to buy low and sale high! When renovating, you do not always want to take the cheap route. Buyers are extremely savvy these days, and they will point out your cheap mistakes at the blink of an eye. Spend money on kitchens and bathrooms, use high quality carpet padding if you install carpet, and make the rooms as uniform as possible. Use neutral paints, uniformed fixtures, and try not to do too much customization. Remember, others will change what is custom to you.

A friend of mine flipped a house once, and he got way in over his head. For starters, he nearly paid market value for the house (which is a no-no). Then, he made custom changes that put him $7,000 over budget. He didn't factor in all of the cost associated with selling the house, such as the agent's commission and the seller's concessions (money paid to help the buyer close the deal). In the end, he lost about $9,500, and he vowed to never flip a house again!

Until this day, I laugh when I think about this scenario. He went in with the mindset of doing it alone. He didn't put together a strong squad to help him move his product. He cut corners, which caused him to pay more to correct his mistakes. He hired workers off

Craigslist® to save money, but they ended up stealing materials and not showing up for work. For the record, many people hire workers from Craigslist® who do exceptional work. Unfortunately, he didn't do his homework on his workers. When it was all said and done, he had to hire a contractor to come in and correct their mistakes. His woes could have been avoided had he positioned himself to win with a good squad and a little more research. NEVER do it alone.

Sometimes, a flip may flop because of the market. You may not be able to sell the property at your projected sales price because of rising interest rates or excessive inventory. This happens. When it does, shift your mindset and deploy the strategies associated with buying and holding. When the market turns back around, sell high! Even the best pushers have to flush dope down the toilet from time to time to avoid jail! Hey, it's the cost of doing business. Just don't put yourself in a position to consistently waste money.

Every great flipper has a horror story. Their resolve is what kept them in the game. When you realize that money is a means to an end, you will press forward and find creative ways to make back your money. Your contractors will put you on to surplus stores that sell products such as flooring and carpet at cheaper rates than you would normally find. Your labor cost may be reduced because your contractor knows that you will bring he or she more work in the future. You may even learn how to do small jobs on Youtube® that will save you hundreds or even thousands of dollars. One of my clients is a general contactor, and he has referred me to some of his subcontractors. On one project, I saved $3,000 on electrical work as a result of this connection! The same subcontractor referred me to a roofer, and I saved $2,000 on my roof. That's $5,000 that I profited on a flip because I had a good squad in place. What could you do with an extra $5,000?

When flips go bad, hang in there! Don't listen to outside voices who wouldn't have the guts to even try a flip. Stick to the squad, dig deep and find a way to come up. A little hustle has never hurt anyone.

Buy and Hold Gone Wrong

Buy and hold projects can also go wrong. One of the most common issues that I've seen is people spending astronomical amounts of money to make repairs for tenants. If the air conditioning unit goes out in the middle of July, you may have to fork over $3,000 for a new unit. The same applies for heaters in January. What happens if a pipe bursts in the middle of the night? Plumbing repairs are expensive, and the insurance deductible alone may dissolve all of your profits for the year. I always recommend that my clients purchase a home warranty through a third party. A good home warranty will cost about $500 annually, but it is well worth it and tax deductible. From a personal experience, I had an air conditioning unit go out at one of my properties in July during a record temperature year. The cost to replace the unit was $4,000, but I only paid a $75 trip fee! The home warranty coverage was a lifesaver! I also had to replace a water heater and a garage door at this same property. I was not so lucky with those costs and I had to come out of pocket $800 for the water heater and $800 for the garage door. For me, that was about 4 months worth of profit, but it was what it was. You win some, and you lose some.

Lastly, home prices may depreciate, preventing you from selling high. When this happens, you simply have to hold the property for a little while longer. This is not always a bad thing. Use your profits to pay down your principle balance, and position yourself to gain more when the market turns back around. Remember, the market ALWAYS turns back around. Be patient, and buy as many properties as possible during down markets. This may be the best time to use owner financing to secure properties. Your profit margin may be lower, but you can combine all of your profits and use them to expedite the payoff of your properties as a whole. What do I mean by that? If you have four properties netting you $400 a month, combine the collective $1,600 and apply that amount to the balance of the property with the lowest payoff.

This is called "snowballing" your payment.

Once you pay off the first loan, you will now have one property that is bringing in 100% gains. So instead of having four properties netting you $400 a month, you now have one property netting you $1,200 and three netting you $400. Your monthly net is now $2,400! You then take that $2,400, apply it to the next lowest balance, and keep repeating this process until all of the loans are paid off. In a matter of years, you'll be netting the full rent on all of your properties! Now that's *Real Dope!*

Even when you lose, you still win! Repairs tend to eat up profits, so get a home warranty. Also, have your home insurance company structure your policy so that you have a low deductible in the event that you have to file a claim. This may raise your montly insurance premium, but it may be well worth it in the end. You'll thank yourself later. At the end of the day, Section 8 will more than likely cover your entire mortgage, so you'll always have that to fall back on. Essentially, your rentals will be on cruise control and all you'll have to do is collect the dough.

PAPER TRAIL

PAPER TRAIL

The one thing that I love about real estate is the paper trial. It's one of the few careers that requires little or no formal education, provides a residual income, and allows you to be a boss while paying taxes! Let's consider the street boss or kingpin. In most mafia movies, this individual rarely goes to jail for murder or drugs. They typically get hit with tax evasion charges. Go figure! The IRS will always get the last laugh, so do what you need to do to keep them out of your business.

The best thing to do is to keep good records. Income generated through the selling and rental of real property is very easy to track. Escrow companies or attorneys orchestrate most home sales, and they provide you with all of the documentation that you will need to file taxes. Section 8 agencies will send you a yearly tax statement for your rental properties. For flips, you typically pay taxes on your gains. If you are an organized person who keeps good records, you can save money by preparing your own taxes with user-friendly tax and bookkeeping software. If you are not so good at keeping records, spend the money and hire an accountant to file your taxes and keep your books. Real estate is just like the dope game when it comes to being taxed. Pay the taxes, and keep it moving! As you become savvier, you will find ways to write off legitimate expenses to reduce your tax burden.

The beauty of paying taxes is that you create a traceable income that will justify your new lifestyle. It is easier to justify that new car, fancy clothes, and exotic trips when you have documented income. The more you document, the easier it will be (for some) to ease away from a "cash lifestyle" and legitimize yourself. Let's face it. This book is called *Real Dope*, and many of the readers are already tied into the dope game. They are looking for a legitimate way out, and real estate can afford them the opportunity to fly straight. What ultimately legitimizes you is paying taxes. It is what it is. Pay the toll, cross the bridge, and get to the other side.

Paying taxes may also put you in a position to obtain credit at a lower interest rate. In this business, credit is good! There is nothing wrong with using someone else's money to build wealth! More income equates to more credit, and more credit creates more opportunities.

With good credit, there is no need for piggybacking or straw purchasing. And with your rental properties in place, you essentially become your own bank! You can refinance your properties and take out the cash equity to buy more houses! You will need at least two years of tax returns to borrow money if you do not already have a W2 source of income.

Many people, who are reading this book, already have a job. Purchasing real estate and using it as an investment will most likely bump you into a new tax bracket. This doesn't necessarily mean that you will have to pay extra taxes. Again, consult a professional or purchase tax software that will do the hard work for you. Whatever you do, PAY YOUR TAXES!

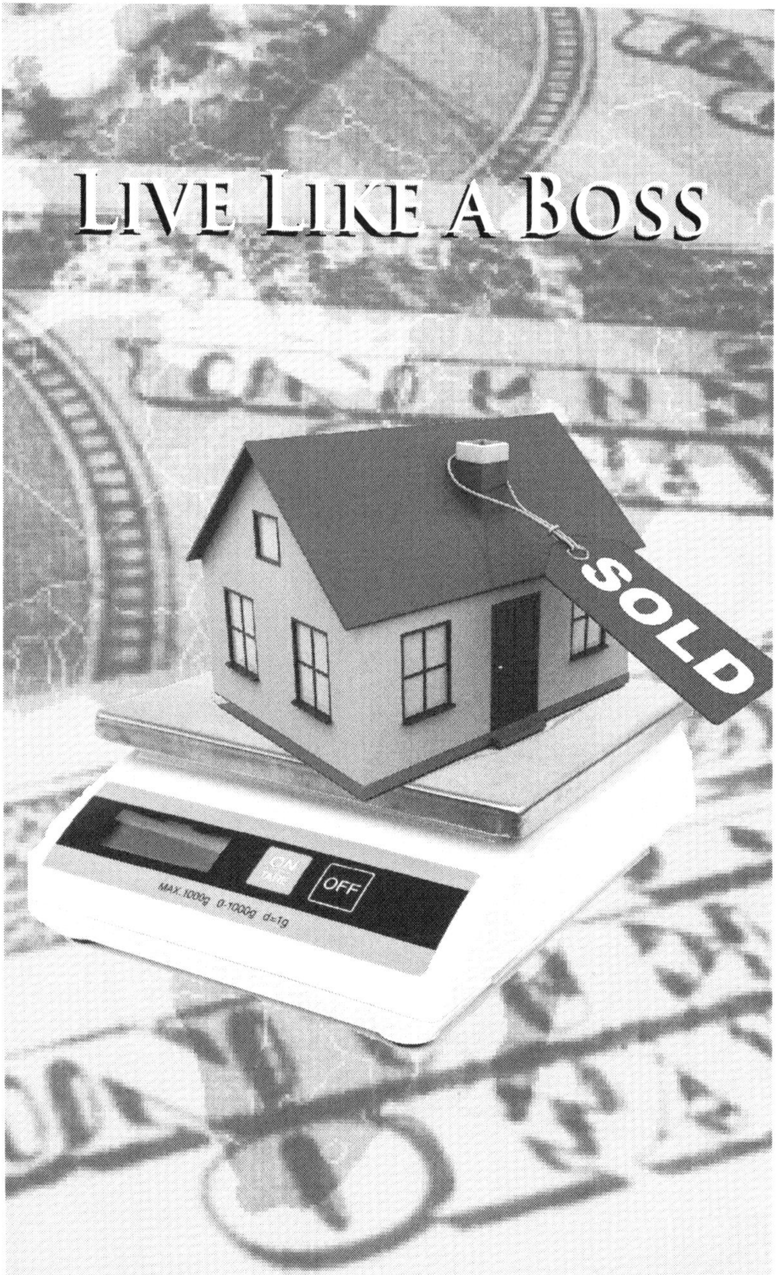
LIVE LIKE A BOSS
SOLD
ON
OFF
MAX.1000g 0-1000g d=1g

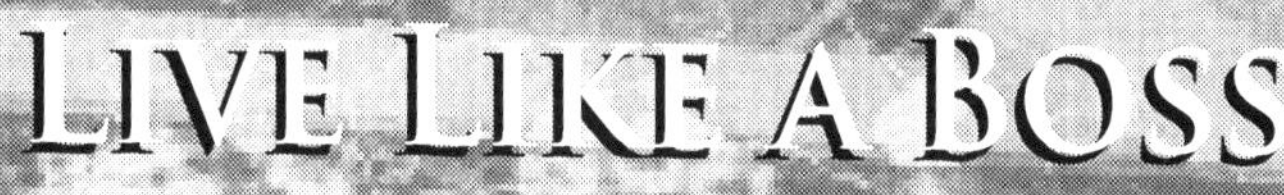

Live Like a Boss

Congratulations! You are officially making boss moves. You have decided to take a chance on you, and I assure you that you will not be disappointed. Real estate and the dope game are paternal twin sisters. They are cut from the same cloth, share similar backgrounds, and have the same effect on people's lives, depending on how you view it. This is your time to live like a boss! You do not realize it now, but you will soon notice the great impact that you will have on the communities in which you choose to invest. Many of the homes that you purchase will be in high crime areas or areas that are viewed as "undesirable."

Sadly, the people in these communities will not be able to see what you see. They won't see the promise that a little "fixing up" can do to a community. They don't see the potential that you see in that small frame house that has served as a trap house for the past three years. Many of your friends will call you crazy for taking this risk. Here is my advice: BE CRAZY!

But be crazy all the way to the bank! If you don't purchase these properties, someone else will. This is a never-ending cycle, and you'll have to get down or lay down! As a real estate broker, I see this vicious cycle everyday, particularly as it relates to renters needing to find a place to stay. At the time of writing this book, there are 10 rental applications for every rental property that is on the market! Owners are getting top dollar and cream-of-the-crop renters. People on Section 8 are having a hard time finding houses to rent because of the stigma associated with Section 8 renters. Listen to me, and listen to me well: Section 8 is guaranteed money! Don't pass it up!

Make real estate your passion. For me, real estate offers endless opportunities. For you, it can do the same. You do not need a license in real estate to make moves. You can live like a boss without a real estate license, a criminal background, and no formal education. FACTS! All you need is a blueprint to get started, and I have provided one for you.

Be goal oriented. My mission is to restore parts of my community through the flipping and leasing of properties. If I can buy a property for $65,000 and raise its value to $130,000, I have done a great service to my community. I have brought light back to the "darkness" of the hood, and in the process I have provided a home to someone in my community that they can be proud of.

I grew up in a section of Dallas that is not known for country clubs and high-end shopping centers. It is known for crime! However, this part of town is slowly changing, and it has a lot to do with the investors coming in and revitalizing my community by purchasing and renovating homes.

I consider it my duty to be a part of this growth, and to provide affordable housing to people who look just like me. In the process, I will gain wealth and teach others how to do the same. Most bosses always tend to give back to their community even though they take a great deal away during the process.

Harsh Reality

HARSH REALITY

Let's face it; the dope game is a bitch! I want to make that perfectly clear. Many lives have been lost through the manufacturing, selling, and distribution of narcotics. Many Black and Latino males have been mass incarcerated due to their involvement in illegal drug activity. Homes have been broken, families shattered, and many children have grown up without their parents due to the influence of drugs. The comparison to the dope game and real estate was necessary because drugs are all around us. They are glamorized in nearly every pop culture song, movie, and television show. Children are taught about the benefits of engaging in a life of drugs without being shown the stark realities that the dope game will have on their lives. I personally know people who have spent years in prison because they wanted to come up quick in the dope game. I know people who have been ambushed and killed because of their involvement in the dope game, and I know people now who can't seem to walk away from this lifestyle.

I also know people who have succumbed to the effects of drug use. Growing up, I had a friend whose mother was strung out on crack. On several occasions, he would come home to find his gaming systems, television, and jewelry missing. His mother would pawn these items for drug money. There were several times when she came to our house at odd hours of the night wanting to borrow $20 to get high. I can only imagine the pain and embarrassment that he felt. I watched a neighbor get hooked on PCP and totally deteriorate. My friend's brother was also in and out of prison his entire life because of his involvement in the distribution and use of drugs. One of my favorite cousins has spent his entire adult life in and out of prison because of his involvement with the dope game.

I often wonder how the lives of my friends and I would have been if our family members invested in real estate rather than narcotics. How different would my life have been if my favorite cousin was home to give me advice face to face rather than through letters? What if our family members would have put their money together to secure properties in our neighborhood? I can hit you with a list of "what if's" for days, but the reality is that you can create The New Narrative ® for your community. You can buy that trap house for pennies on the dollar, convert it to a rental property, and run off the gangs in your community. You can literally own an entire neighborhood, jack up the property value, sale high and collect! The best part of it all… it's legal!

Take a chance on you and be the boss that you were meant to be. Economic empowerment! Now that's *Real Dope!*

About the Author

Tim Jackson was born and raised in the Pleasant Grove sector of Dallas, TX. A graduate of Dallas Independent School District's Skyline High School and The University of Texas at Dallas, Tim is deeply rooted in his community, where he serves as the president of the R.E.A.L. Youth Mentoring Program." Tim is focused on partnering with individuals and companies to educate African Americans on the importance of home ownership and credit consciousness. Tim also understands the importance of creating a new narrative that is associated with African Americans, particularly African American men. Tim firmly believes that the narrative associated with African American men will completely change for the better, and he orders his steps in such a way to effectively BE that change while encouraging other men to do the same.

Made in the USA
San Bernardino, CA
27 May 2017